ACTION EVENTS

DRAG

RACING

ACTION EVENTS

DRAG
RACING

BY JEFF SAVAGE

CRESTWOOD HOUSE
Parsippany, New Jersey

Photo Credits
Cover Photo Credits by—Motorsports Marketing Inc.
Cover and book design by Liz Kril
Copyright ©1997 by Silver Burdett Press

 Published by Crestwood House,
A Division of Simon & Schuster,
299 Jefferson Road, Parsippany, NJ 07054

First Edition
Printed in the United States of America
10 9 8 7 6 5 4 3 2 1

Library of Congress Cataloging-in-Publication Data

Savage, Jeff, 1961-

    Drag racing/by Jeff Savage.—1st ed.

        p. cm. —(Action events)

    Includes index.

Summary: Covers the great drivers and races in drag racing history as well as the basic structures, rules, and dangers of this motorsport.

ISBN 0-89686-890-7 (lib. bdg.)—ISBN 0-382-39293-0 (pbk.)

1. Drag racing—Juvenile literature. [1. Drag racing.] I. Title. II. Series: Savage, Jeff, 1961-   Action events.
GV1029.3.S38 1997
796.7'2—dc20   95-32759

#PRO
6
Bob Glidden

Ford

uality Care

FORD

MERCURY

LINCOLN

QC
QC

Competition Cams & Lifters

NO FEAR

CONTENTS

1 A RACE BETWEEN FATHER AND SON 10

2 DRAG RACING BEGINS 14

3 THE DRAGSTERS 18

4 GREEN MEANS GO! 22

5 THE SNAKE 24

6 VETERAN RACERS 28

7   LEARNING FROM DAD .32

8   BEATING THE BOYS 34

9   THE GREAT DRIVERS 40

10 JUNIOR DRAGSTERS 42

    GLOSSARY 44

    INDEX 48

CHAPTER 1

A Race Between Father and Son

Ba Rup. Ba Rup. Ba Rup. Ba Rup. The shiny chrome engine gurgles as the sleek red dragster creeps to the starting line. Inside the cockpit, the driver is tightly strapped in and is wearing a red helmet and fireproof suit. He stares straight ahead down the quarter-mile track. It's Connie Kalitta, the veteran driver from Ypsilanti, Michigan. He's about to race in the final of the 1994 Gatornationals at Gainesville Raceway in northern Florida. *Ba Rup. Ba Rup. Ba Rup.*

Connie glances over to his left at his competitor. Sunk low behind the **roll bar** in the cockpit of the opposing red dragster is Scott Kalitta—Connie's son!

None of the 55,000 fans who have jammed Gainesville Raceway would have predicted this. It's the first father-son final in the history of **top fuel** drag racing. The sun is bright. The wind is calm. It's a perfect day for racing. Scott looks back at his dad and his heart swells with pride. Scott wouldn't even be a drag racer if it weren't for Connie.

The key to racing Top Fuel dragsters is reaction time—watching for the green light and then shooting off the starting line. Connie began racing in the early 1960s. He had lost an eye in an accident when he was 18

SCOTT KALITTA (FOREGROUND) AND HIS FATHER, CONNIE, ROAR DOWN THE TRACK SIDE BY SIDE.

years old. But Connie met the physical challenge of seeing with just one eye by becoming a top racer on the National Hot Rod Association (NHRA) circuit.

Connie also was an expert **mechanic** who worked as the crew chief for Shirley Muldowney, the legendary female drag racer. Connie spent long days in hot-rod shops, and Scott was always at his father's side with a wrench in hand. Scott was thrilled to be a young member of Shirley's crew in 1977 when she became the only woman to win the NHRA points championship.

The one thing Scott enjoyed more than helping his father work on engines was watching him race. Scott loved to see the powerful engines spit fire and spew smoke as they tore up the track. Connie taught Scott how to drive—how to grip the butterfly-shaped steering wheel, how to release the brake, how to propel the dragster down the track at breakneck speed. And eventually Scott began racing.

So here they were, father and son, side by side, ready to race. *Ba Rup. Ba Rup. Ba Rup.*

The two Kalittas had gone head-to-head four times before but never in the final event. Connie had won

three times against his son. Scott had won once. But Scott's win had come just two weeks earlier in the semifinals of an event at Houston Raceway Park in Texas. In that race, Scott recorded the fastest time ever in drag racing—it took him only 4.726 seconds to travel the entire quarter mile. His dragster looked like a red blur as it whizzed past the fans.

Ba Rup. Ba Rup. Ba Rup. Scott presses slightly on the **accelerator** as thousands of horsepower wait ready in his fuel-injected engine. Scott became the fastest man in motorsports a year earlier when he ripped through a race at 305.18 miles per hour to beat Kenny Bernstein. He was in first place in the NHRA yearly point standings again in 1994. Scott definitely has the faster dragster. And Connie knows it.

But Connie has the experience. He's been in a title race dozens of times throughout his long career. He's cool and steady. The only problem is that he hasn't raced much in the last couple of years because he's been involved with his airplane business. And he hasn't actually won an event in eight years. Connie is definitely the underdog.

The stage indicator lights flash, signaling that the race is about to start. The enormous crowd shouts encouragement. Scott and Connie focus on a post of lights above them known as the **Christmas Tree**. The amber lights come on, the engines are revving, the green light flicks on, and *BAAA-RROOOOOM*

the drivers take off at full blast. Down the track they come, side by side—*EEEEEYYOOWWW!* To the finish line they speed . . . and the winner is . . . Connie! A **parachute** blossoms out behind each dragster to stop it as the crowd roars with delight.

"To race against your son in a class where everyone is so awesome is pretty neat," Connie says as he raises the winner's trophy. "I'd have to say this is the highlight of my career."

Scott is disappointed that he didn't win, but he knows he can't win every time. When he does lose, it may as well be to his father. "This is neat for us, having the camaraderie and the competition," Scott says afterward. "It adds a lot of spice to the racing. Just seeing my dad win is great."

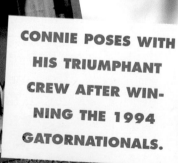

CONNIE POSES WITH HIS TRIUMPHANT CREW AFTER WINNING THE 1994 GATORNATIONALS.

Chapter 2

Drag Racing Begins

Drag racing has come a long way from its uncertain beginnings on America's back roads and city streets. Today it is a celebrated sport conducted on smooth asphalt surfaces in cars outfitted with modern safety equipment. Millions of people attend these organized races each year. It has long been a popular event—but it hasn't always been legal.

Drag racing began on the city streets of southern California in the late 1930s. Cars were being developed into powerful machines, and drivers were eager to test the power of these machines. The drivers were usually young men willing to risk injury by racing. They would pull up beside one another at a stop sign and exchange knowing glances. Then they would stomp down on their accelerator pedals and screech away down the street. Stoplights were even better than signs as the green light served as a perfect signal to start the race.

Rods are an important part of an engine, and drivers who beefed up their engine for more power began calling their cars "hot rods." When a driver popped the clutch and tromped on the accelerator, the car's front end often would spring into the air in what is known as a **wheelie**. As the car would roar ahead with its front end raised, its back end would drag along the ground. This is how the term *drag racing* originated.

Drag racing became more dangerous as young drivers raced each other from stoplight to stoplight. Crashes were common as drivers underestimated the power of their engines. Teenagers were getting hurt. Parents were furious and soon the police clamped down.

They put more officers on the streets and cited drag racers for speeding, reckless driving, and other offenses. So drivers began to sneak off to secluded areas where they could test their engines. Even though police often arrived to break up these secret contests, they couldn't quell the desire of young Americans to race.

Responsible adults knew they had to do something. This racing fad just wasn't going to end. The adults decided to organize these drag races by providing supervision. Stretches of roads were marked off for youngsters to test the limits of their cars. Airports sometimes arranged for the use of a runway for a few hours. Events were held on dry lake beds and desert areas that were flat for long stretches. The most famous of these was the Bonneville Salt Flats in Utah. It remains a popular racing site today.

Neighborhood hot-rod clubs were formed. Groups of kids would meet at automotive garages to work on their dragsters and discuss the virtues of different kinds of tires and engine parts. Millions of car enthusiasts soon were sharing their common interest.

TOP FUEL DRIVERS SIT LOW IN THE COCKPIT UNDER A ROLL BAR AND WEAR PROTECTIVE CLOTHING.

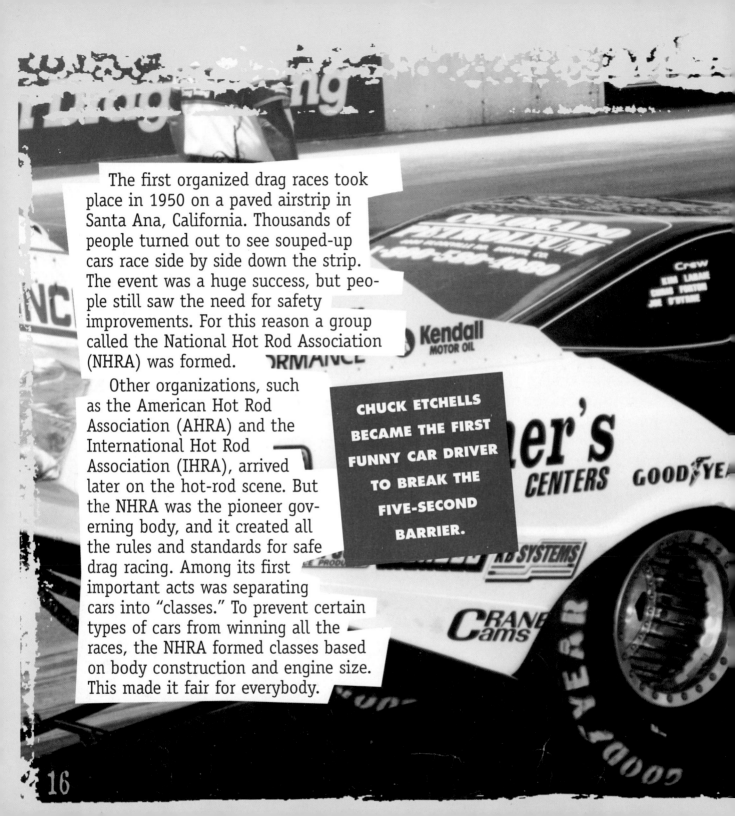

The first organized drag races took place in 1950 on a paved airstrip in Santa Ana, California. Thousands of people turned out to see souped-up cars race side by side down the strip. The event was a huge success, but people still saw the need for safety improvements. For this reason a group called the National Hot Rod Association (NHRA) was formed.

Other organizations, such as the American Hot Rod Association (AHRA) and the International Hot Rod Association (IHRA), arrived later on the hot-rod scene. But the NHRA was the pioneer governing body, and it created all the rules and standards for safe drag racing. Among its first important acts was separating cars into "classes." To prevent certain types of cars from winning all the races, the NHRA formed classes based on body construction and engine size. This made it fair for everybody.

CHUCK ETCHELLS BECAME THE FIRST FUNNY CAR DRIVER TO BREAK THE FIVE-SECOND BARRIER.

PRO STOCK CARS ARE AMONG THE FASTEST IN THE WORLD.

CHAPTER 3

THE DRAGSTERS

There are over 100 classes of dragsters today. The three most popular classes are Top Fuel, **Pro Stock**, and **Funny Cars**. Other classes include Top Alcohol Dragsters, Top Alcohol Funny Cars, Super Stock, Super Comp, Super Gas, and Stock Eliminator. Technology is so advanced that most dragster engines are now designed by computers. That's quite a change from the past.

Dick Kraft is thought to have built the first dragster. In 1948, Dick gave his roadster the look of a dune buggy by removing much of the car's body. He then raced it to speeds of nearly 100 miles per hour.

In the mid-1950s, Mickey Thompson created the first modern dragster by placing the engine over the huge rear wheels. Then he put the driver's cage behind the engine so that almost all the weight was over the back wheels. This

THE SLEEK BODY OF THE TOP FUEL DRAGSTER HELPS MAKE IT THE FASTEST RACING CAR EVER.

improved the dragster's **traction**. Traction is the ability of the tires to grip the road without slipping. The better the traction, the faster the tires can turn and push the car along without spinning out. But as more weight was shifted to the rear, Mickey's dragster began to rise up in the front—and sometimes even flipped over. The body of the dragster was lengthened to provide balance. Devices called **spoilers** were added to the front and back of Mickey's vehicle to change the air-flow and decrease lift.

Mickey's new dragster, with its tiny front and long body, became known as the **slingshot**. Suddenly, Mickey became unbeatable. To catch up with him, racers had to build their own long, sleek dragsters.

"Big Daddy" Don Garlits made the most recent major change to dragsters when he moved the engine behind the driver in the early 1970s. Don made this change because he was concerned about the safety of the drivers. Don's car, known as the Swamp Rat, became so famous that it was later enshrined in the Smithsonian Institution.

Because of pioneers like Mickey Thompson and Don Garlits, Top Fuel dragsters can reach greater speeds and accelerate faster than any other racing vehicle on earth. They are powered by fuel-injected, 5,000-horsepower engines that burn a fuel called **nitromethane.**

By contrast, Pro Stock racers resemble cars you see on the streets and highways. But there are plenty of differences. Their engines burn gasoline but are rebuilt to provide supercharged power. The **chassis** and suspension are modified. And, of course, the tires are much bigger.

Funny Cars are shaped like normal cars, but their bodies are made of fiberglass, which is much lighter than metal. They have a powerful engine similar to Top Fuel dragsters and can go nearly as fast. They are called funny cars because a racing announcer thought they "looked funny" when he first saw them.

So you want to buy a racing car? The best cars today, especially the Top Fuel dragsters, cost as much as $500,000 for the frame and body and another $250,000 for the engine. Then don't forget all the money it takes to keep the machine in perfect running condition. That's why most drag racers are amateurs—they can't afford to be professionals.

COMPANIES SPONSOR DRIVERS LIKE CORY McCLENATHAN IN RETURN FOR ADVERTISING.

Chapter 4

Green Means Go!

By now you've probably figured out the basic structure of drag racing. Two cars line up side by side. At a precise signal, they take off down a short, straight track. The first one to cross the finish line wins.

Unlike Indy car or NASCAR racing, in which a group of cars races around the track at once, drag racing has always been between two contestants. There is one winner and one loser. In most cases the loser is eliminated from competition while the winner advances to the next round. Eventually only one car remains and is declared the champion.

The track size remains the same, no matter what class of cars is competing. The distance from start to finish was established in the 1950s as one quarter of a mile (1,320 feet). Why a quarter of a mile? Because on an airstrip, a quarter mile was the maximum distance a car could go and still have enough pavement to allow the car to come to a stop. Also, a car couldn't travel much farther at top speed without the engine overheating or blowing up.

The set of lights at the starting line is called a Christmas Tree. Amber-colored lights flash, followed by the green light at the bottom of the column of lights. If a driver starts before the green, the red light flashes to signal a foul and the driver is disqualified.

The NHRA Drag Racing Series features 18 events each year. Among the biggest are the Winternationals at Pomona

AN AVERAGE OF 92,000 FANS JAM THE STADIUMS AT EACH EVENT TO SEE THEIR FAVORITE RACERS.

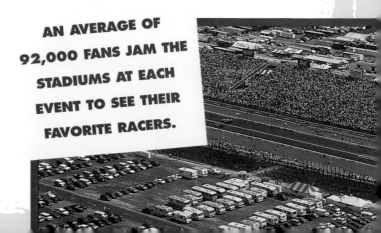

Raceway in southern California; the Southern Nationals in Atlanta, Georgia; the Mile-High Nationals in Denver, Colorado; the U.S. Nationals at Indianapolis, Indiana; and the Select Finals at the end of the year in Pomona.

Thousands of people attend these events. Total attendance at the 18 events has grown each year for the last decade. The series broke the one-million mark in 1987. By 1993 the figure swelled to 1,649,178. That's an average of almost 92,000 fans at each of the 18 events. The two-million mark is not far off.

Drivers in each of the classes receive points for their performance at each of the races. The points are added up at the end of the year to determine who has the most points, who finished second, and so on.

More than $2 million in prize money is awarded by the NHRA, and over $27 million is awarded by **sponsors**! Sponsors are companies who con-tribute money in return for the advertising of their products. Some big

sponsors are oil companies, automotive parts companies, fast-food chains, and American car companies.

Drivers also receive sponsorship money from companies in return for wearing the company's logo on their racing uniforms and plastering it all over their dragsters. For example, racers Cory McClenathan and Cruz Pedregon are sponsored by McDonald's. So everywhere Cory and Cruz go, the "golden arches" of McDonald's are sure to follow. Cory and Cruz even appear in advertisements for their sponsor, eating McDonald's french fries.

Over 26,000 people in the country have a license to race in competition. But only a handful, like Cory and Cruz, are superstars.

23

CHAPTER 5

THE SNAKE

Don "The Snake" Prudhomme couldn't believe his ears. He was listening to a sports talk show on the radio one day while driving home. Caller after caller was saying that Don should retire. The legendary driver had announced a week earlier that the upcoming 1994 season would be his final year on the racing circuit. But sports fans were saying, "Why bother?" They thought The Snake had lost his bite, that he was too slow for the competition. They said he had no chance of winning another race.

Granted, things had gone badly for Don the previous year. He didn't win at any of the 18 Top Fuel events on the circuit. He never even made it to the final round. He wound up fourteenth in the overall points standings—his lowest finish ever. But washed up? Too old? No chance of winning?

No way.

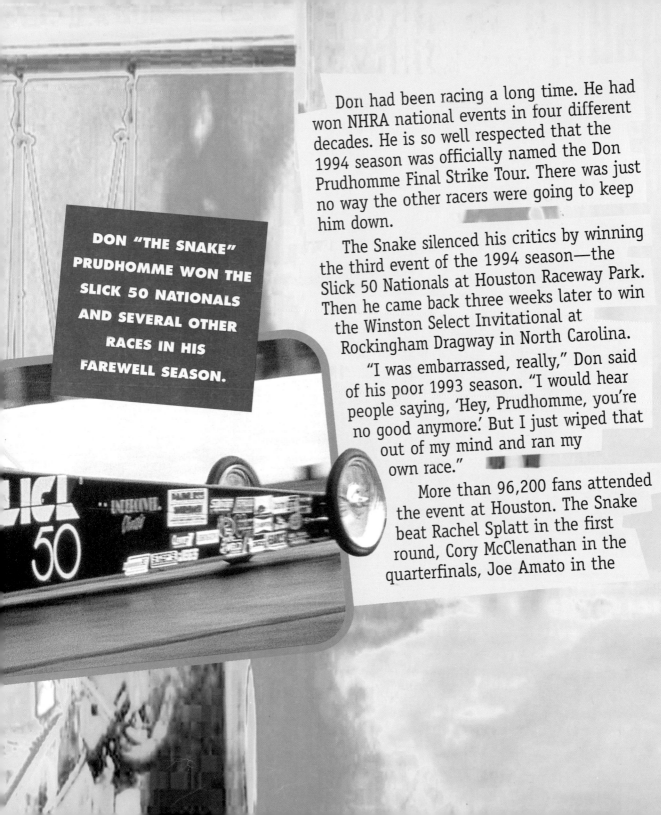

Don had been racing a long time. He had won NHRA national events in four different decades. He is so well respected that the 1994 season was officially named the Don Prudhomme Final Strike Tour. There was just no way the other racers were going to keep him down.

The Snake silenced his critics by winning the third event of the 1994 season—the Slick 50 Nationals at Houston Raceway Park. Then he came back three weeks later to win the Winston Select Invitational at Rockingham Dragway in North Carolina.

"I was embarrassed, really," Don said of his poor 1993 season. "I would hear people saying, 'Hey, Prudhomme, you're no good anymore.' But I just wiped that out of my mind and ran my own race."

More than 96,200 fans attended the event at Houston. The Snake beat Rachel Splatt in the first round, Cory McClenathan in the quarterfinals, Joe Amato in the semifinals, and Scott Kalitta in the finals. "It's difficult to explain how this feels," Don said in the victory circle. "Things haven't gone our way for such a long time. We've been down, beat up. I sure needed a win. The crew needed it, too."

In front of 77,000 spectators at Rockingham, Don swept through the field again to become the first two-time winner of 1994. He beat Cory McClenathan in the final when Cory **red-lighted** (left the starting line before the green light flashed). Don thought something was strange when Cory shot out so fast. "When he left and we were going down the track, I said, 'Man, this cat cut a light. There is no way I'm going to catch him,' " Don said. "He was so far ahead of

me, I was just riding along, listening to my motor."

Don discovered he'd won the race when he crossed the finish line and saw his win light on the guardrail. "That shows how bad my luck is," Don joked. "Things are finally beginning to happen for me, and I'm retiring."

The triumphant 1994 season was a great ending to an amazing motorsports career for Don Prudhomme. He started racing while in his teens when he joined a car club in Burbank, California. He amassed a 230-7 win-loss record as a teenager. He won four straight Funny Car yearly points championships and dozens of other titles. Thousands of adoring fans were sad to see The Snake finally slither away. Not so the other drivers. They had been bitten long enough.

> **QUOTE**
> "Things are finally beginning to happen for me..."

TOP FUEL
DRAGSTERS
GO SO FAST
THAT THEY'RE
SOMETIMES
BOUND TO
CRASH.

27

Chapter 6

Veteran Racers

Sports like basketball and football require a totally fit body, and the majority of athletes retire before they reach the age of 40. That's not the case in drag racing. Certain physical requirements such as quick reaction time and good hand-eye coordination are needed to race. But things like endurance and leg strength that fade as our bodies grow older are not necessary in motorsports—especially one in which the race is over in about six seconds.

Eddie Hill proved in 1993 that age is just a number as he captured his first NHRA yearly championship at the age of 57. Eddie won a record six events in his car, the Nuclear Banana. He clinched the points title in the next-to-last event of the year in Dallas, despite losing in the first round. With dozens of reporters and photographers assembled for the press conference afterward, Eddie hugged his wife, Ercie, and began to cry. "I was in shock, too choked up even to talk," Eddie remembered. "Ercie had to do my talking for me."

Eddie is a favorite among racing fans because he is so approachable. He lets spectators come down to the pits to examine the Nuclear Banana and play with Hot Dog, his pet dog. People constantly ask him why he continues to race even after turning 60. Eddie always has the same answer. "Because," he says, "I love speed." He began racing at age 11 on a motor scooter. Then he became a powerboat racer and set several speed records even though he didn't know how to swim. He crashed several

EDDIE'S FRONT END IS OFF THE GROUND. HIS DRAGSTER WILL FLIP IN THIS RACE, BUT EDDIE WILL WALK AWAY FROM THE CRASH.

times in boats and had to be pulled from the water. It's a good thing that Eddie discovered dragsters!

Another veteran driver is Kenny Bernstein, the first drag racer to go faster than 300 miles per hour. The King, as he is known, broke the 300-mph barrier in 1992 at the Gatornationals in Gainesville, Florida. Kenny celebrated his fiftieth birthday in 1994, and he continues to compete full-time.

EDDIE HILL WON HIS FIRST DRAG-RACING CHAMPI-ONSHIP AT THE AGE OF 57.

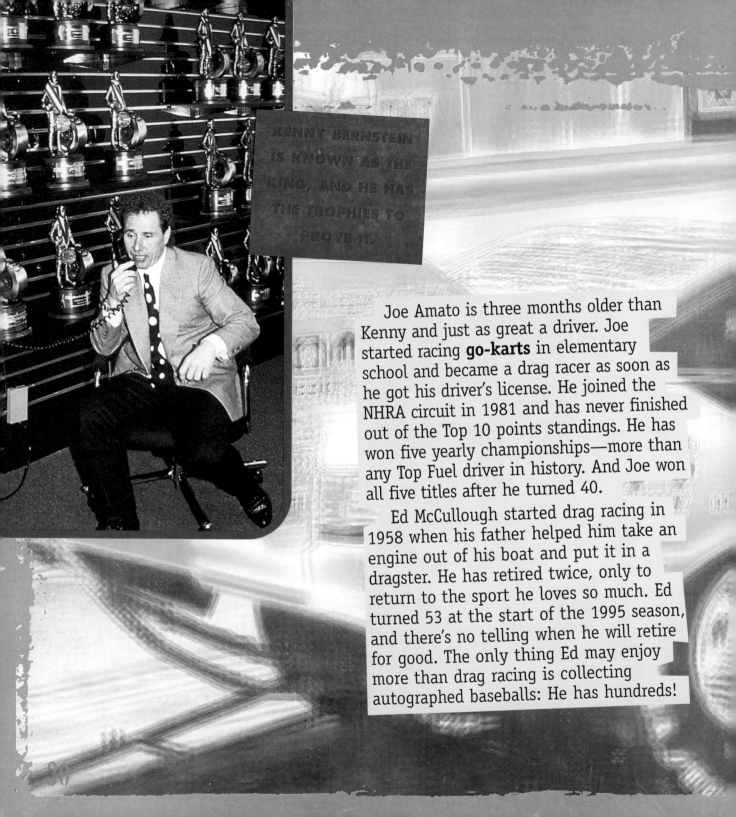

Joe Amato is three months older than Kenny and just as great a driver. Joe started racing **go-karts** in elementary school and became a drag racer as soon as he got his driver's license. He joined the NHRA circuit in 1981 and has never finished out of the Top 10 points standings. He has won five yearly championships—more than any Top Fuel driver in history. And Joe won all five titles after he turned 40.

Ed McCullough started drag racing in 1958 when his father helped him take an engine out of his boat and put it in a dragster. He has retired twice, only to return to the sport he loves so much. Ed turned 53 at the start of the 1995 season, and there's no telling when he will retire for good. The only thing Ed may enjoy more than drag racing is collecting autographed baseballs: He has hundreds!

One of the autographed balls Ed has is from former slugger Jack Clark. Jack sees Ed at every racing event. Jack retired from baseball in 1992 and became a drag racer. He bashed 340 home runs for the San Francisco Giants and St. Louis Cardinals before he stopped playing baseball. But Jack still was an athlete at heart. He still had the desire to compete in a sport.

He chose racing because he knew he could compete into the twenty-first century. "When I was a Little Leaguer, I never thought I could make it to the major leagues and play professional baseball," Jack said. "Seeing the drag races as a kid, I never thought I would be out there racing. I've been fortunate to fulfill both of my dreams."

31

CHAPTER 7

LEARNING FROM DAD

Connie and Scott Kalitta have thrilled fans with many memorable battles over the years. But they were not the first father-son duo to meet in a professional drag-race final. That honor goes to the Johnsons—father Warren and son Kurt.

Warren already was racing when his son was born in 1963. Kurt remembers playing with his toy race cars while riding in the back seat of the family car as his father and his mother, Arlene, drove from event to event. By the time Kurt was 10, his father was teaching him about engines. Soon Kurt didn't go anywhere without a wrench in his hand. He watched Warren roar to victory many times over the years, but he knew his father was frustrated over not winning the Pro Stock yearly points championship. Warren finished second in the points standings six different times in a 15-year period. And each runner-up finish was more agonizing than the last.

In 1992, after another second-place finish the year before, Warren exploded off the starting line like never before. He won eight national events to finally capture the Pro Stock points championship just before his fiftieth birthday. Kurt was a key member of Warren's crew at the time. "Up until then there was no time to even think about racing," Kurt remembered. "I was an engine builder and the head machinist. I had too many other responsibilities."

But now that Warren had finally won the most coveted prize in drag racing, Kurt told his father that he wanted to become a drag racer. Warren was thrilled, and Kurt joined the circuit in 1993. But excitement quickly turned to horror as Warren and Arlene saw their son suffer a terrifying crash in the second event of the year at the Motorcraft-Ford Nationals in Phoenix. In a third-round race against Larry Morgan, Kurt lost control of his Oldsmobile Cutlass and it slid sideways toward the retaining wall. The car slammed against the wall with such force that it flipped up and over the

wall. It came to a stop in muddy water. Miraculously, Kurt was not hurt. He was strapped in so well that his restraining belts saved him.

Kurt lost in the first round in the next event, and people whispered that maybe the crash had ruined his confidence. Kurt proved that wasn't the case two events later when he reached the final of the Southern Nationals in Atlanta. His opponent? Warren Johnson. The Atlanta Dragway stands were packed as more than 88,000 fans watched Warren edge his son at the finish line in the first father-son final in drag-racing history.

Kurt was good enough to reach an event final seven times in that storybook rookie season. Six of the seven times his opponent was his father. Kurt won three times and was named drag racing Rookie of the Year. Warren did even better—winning nine events to claim his second straight points championship. Asked what was most special about the year, Warren said, "I especially enjoyed seeing the success of my son."

Chapter 8

Beating the Boys

It sometimes isn't easy for a woman to break into an arena dominated by men. Some of the men may be protective of their "turf" and quick to taunt and tease the woman. "You can't do what we do," they say. "You're just a woman." How foolish these men look.

Shelly Anderson became the fourth woman to win an NHRA national event when she defeated Mike Dunn in 1993 at the Keystone Nationals in Reading, Pennsylvania. Rachel Splatt was right behind Shelly, becoming the fifth woman to win a Top Fuel event. Before Shelly and Rachel were Lori Johns from Corpus Christi, Texas, and Lucille Lee from Long Beach, California. But the woman who broke the gender barrier, the woman who boldly invaded the all-male world of drag racing, was Shirley Muldowney.

Shirley burst onto the racing scene at just the right time. It was the early 1970s, when powerful forces of women in America were demanding equal rights. Shirley immediately became a symbol for their cause. Then in 1977 she rocked the auto-racing world by capturing the NHRA points championship. Afterward, she uttered her famous phrase, "I love beating the boys." Some male competitors were embarrassed to lose to a woman and reacted in a hostile manner. Shirley had created quite a stir.

The woman from Mount Clemens, Michigan, kept right on winning in her Top Fuel dragster. Shirley won the points title again in 1980 to become the first two-time yearly champion—man or woman! She became the first three-time champion

SHELLY ANDERSON BECAME THE FOURTH WOMAN EVER TO WIN AN NHRA EVENT.

SHIRLEY
MULDOWNEY
BURST ONTO THE
RACING SCENE AT
THE RIGHT TIME.

by winning again in 1982. By now she had gained the respect of most of her male competitors—not all of them, but most of them. "I love drag racing and I love beating the boys at a game they think is their own," she said once again.

Shirley hasn't competed at national events for several years, but she continues to race her Top Fuel dragster in local matches. Naturally she was the first woman elected to the Motorsports Hall of Fame in Michigan. And a respected media firm recently reported that the top three names in all of racing are A. J. Foyt, Richard Petty, and Shirley Muldowney. She will forever be remembered as a great pioneer in motorsports.

SHIRLEY IS A THREE-TIME CHAMPION AND A FAN FAVORITE.

CHAPTER 9

THE GREAT DRIVERS

In many professional sports, one team seems to dominate for a few years in a row. The Chicago Bulls won the NBA (National Basketball Association) title three straight years. The Buffalo Bills played in four straight Super Bowls. The Oakland A's won three straight World Series. It is no different in drag racing. In the Top Fuel class, Don Garlits dominated in the early 1970s. Then came Shirley Muldowney, Darrell Gwynn, and Joe Amato. Joe won the points title in 1984 and again in 1988. But it wasn't until the 1990s that he began to dominate. Joe won the championship three straight years before his streak was snapped in 1993. He began racing at age 11 in go-karts in his hometown of Old Forge, Pennsylvania. He has been racing ever since. "I love to feel the power of the engine as it roars down the track," Joe says. "I want to race forever."

It may take Joe that long to catch the all-time points title champion. Joe is second in history with five drag racing titles. But he's well behind the leader— Bob Glidden. Bob has won an amazing 10 points titles in the Pro Stock class. Bob is from Whiteland, Indiana, where at age 14 he learned about engines when he began fixing the family tractor.

There is plenty of competition these days for Joe Amato and Bob Glidden. In the Pro Stock class, Jerry Eckman of Newark, Ohio, knows all about speed. He was a guided missile vehicle operator in Europe before he started racing.

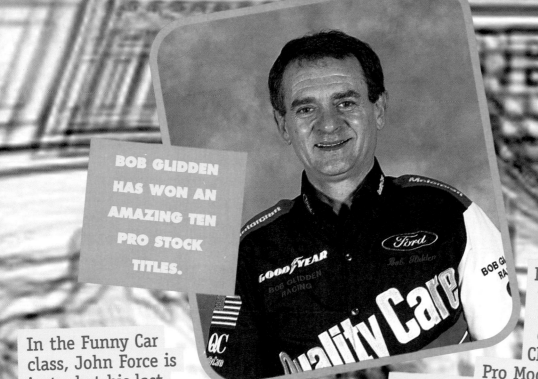

In the Funny Car class, John Force is just what his last name says—a force. John won four Funny Car titles in five years in the 1990s, and there's no telling when he'll stop. Among the Funny Car drivers trying to catch John are veteran Chuck Etchells of Putnam, Connecticut; car collector Al Hoffmann of Umatilla, Florida; and "Flash" Gordon Mineo of Rockwall, Texas, who has been driving Funny Cars since 1967.

The International Hot Rod Association (IHRA) also features some terrific racers. Big Chuck Peterson from Dakota Dunes, South Dakota, drives the world's fastest super-charged 1969 Chevelle in the Pro Modified class.

Chuck's son, Chad Peterson, joined the IHRA circuit in 1992, won three events, and was named Rookie of the Year.

The list of great drivers goes on. There's Scott Geoffrion, Larry Morgan, Mark Pawuk, Edmond Richardson, Rickie Smith, Bruce Allen, Randy Anderson, Tom Hoover, Scotty Richardson, Kenji Okazaki, Steve Johnson, Jim Epler, and many more. Drag racing certainly will never run out of drivers.

Chapter 10
Junior Dragsters

Where do the great drag racers come from? It's simple. The Junior Drag Racing League.

Thousands of children across the country compete in the Junior Drag Racing League sponsored by the National Hot Rod Association. It is a safe and fun way to learn about the sport of drag racing.

Children compete in small-sized dragsters in three separate classes. The Minor class is for kids ages 8–9. This class competes on a track one eighth of a mile long, or half the distance of pro tracks. The Major class and the Open class are for kids ages 10–17. The Open class is more difficult but both classes compete on a quarter-mile track just like the pros.

You don't have to be a great driver with lots of experience to win in the Junior Drag Racing League. Amanda Tucker competed in her first race at Rockingham Dragway in North Carolina against other 13-year-old children—and she won! "I came home with the trophy from my very first race, and you should have seen the smile on my daddy's face," she said. And Amanda is just one of many first-time winners.

Junior Dragsters are run almost every weekend at racetracks—big and small—throughout the country. And most tracks have a points program in which the top 10 finishers get to compete at the championship at Indianapolis Raceway Park each summer. That's not the Top 10 kids in the country—that's the Top 10 kids at each track! Who knows who will be the next Don "The Snake" Prudhomme or Shirley Muldowney?

See you at the track.

DRAG-RACING CARS ARE GETTING MORE POWERFUL ALL THE TIME.

GLOSSARY

accelerator The foot pedal used to control the speed of a vehicle

chassis The frame, wheels, and machinery that support a dragster

Christmas Tree The system of lights at the starting line that signal the start of the race

Funny Car A dragster with a stock (standard) body and a powerful Top Fuel engine

go-kart A small motorized vehicle driven mostly by children

mechanic The person who performs repairs and fine-tuning on the dragster

nitromethane A type of fuel used by some dragsters

parachute A cloth device that blossoms out behind a dragster to help slow it down

Pro Stock A dragster that has a stock (standard) body and runs on pump gasoline

red-light To commit a violation of the rules by leaving the starting line too early

roll bar The sturdy metal bar mounted above the driver for protection

slingshot A dragster with a small front end and an extra long body

spoiler The device mounted on a dragster to alter air flow and decrease lift

sponsor A person or company that provides financial support to a competitor

Top Fuel A sleek dragster powered by nitromethane instead of gasoline.

traction The ability of tires to grip the road without slipping

wheelie A maneuver in which the front end of a vehicle rises into the air

INDEX

Amato, Joe 25, 30, 40
American Hot Rod Association (AHRA) 16
Anderson, Shelly 34

Bernstein, Kenny 12, 29
Bonneville Salt Flats 15

Christmas Tree 13, 22
Clark, Jack 31
costs 21
crashes 32, 33

Dunn, Mike 34

Eckman, Jerry 40
Etchells, Chuck 41

Force, John 41
Foyt, A. J. 38
Funny Cars 18, 21, 26, 41

Garlits, Don "Big Daddy" 20, 21, 40
Glidden, Bob 40
Gwynn, Darrell 40

Hill, Eddie 28, 29
Hoffmann, Al 41

International Hot Rod Association (IHRA) 16, 41

Johns, Lori 34
Johnson, Kurt 32, 33
Johnson, Warren 32, 33
Junior Drag Racing League 42, 43

Kalitta, Connie 10, 11, 12, 13, 32
Kalitta, Scott 10, 11, 12, 13, 26, 32
Kraft, Dick 18

Lee, Lucille 34

McClenathan, Cory 23, 25, 26
McCullough, Ed 30, 31
Mineo, "Flash" Gordon 41
Morgan, Larry 32
Motorsports Hall of Fame 38
Muldowney, Shirley 11, 34, 38, 40

National Hot Rod Association (NHRA) 11, 16, 25, 30, 42
NHRA Drag Racing Series 22, 23
Nuclear Banana 28

origins 14, 15, 16, 18

Pedregon, Cruz 23
Peterson, Big Chuck 41
Peterson, Chad 41
Petty, Richard 38
points titles 11, 12, 23, 26, 28, 30, 32, 33, 34, 40, 41
prize money 23
Pro Stock 18, 21, 32, 40
Prudhomme, Don "The Snake" 24, 25, 26

rules 16, 22

slingshot 20
Splatt, Rachel 25, 34
sponsors 23
Swamp Rat 20

Thompson, Mickey 18, 19, 20, 21
Top Fuel 10, 18, 21, 24, 30, 34, 38, 40
Tucker, Amanda 42, 43

women racers 11, 25, 34